Lancashire Dream Weavers

Edited By Warren Arthur

First published in Great Britain in 2017 by:

Young Writers
Remus House
Coltsfoot Drive
Peterborough
PE2 9BF
Telephone: 01733 890066
Website: www.youngwriters.co.uk

FOREWORD

Welcome Readers!
Dreams play a big role in our life, whether from the worlds that keep us entertained at night to the dreams and ambitions we aspire to in the future, so it was only fitting we used this as our topic for our latest nationwide primary school competition.

I am proud to present 'Once Upon A Dream – Lancashire Dream Weavers', a collection of poetic treasures that will make your imaginations run wild. Among these pages you will find a variety of poetic styles, from dream acrostics to candy land couplets to fear provoking free verse. Some poems may leave you jumping for joy, some may tickle your sides, while others may pull at your heart strings as each author becomes their own dream catcher.

The selection process, while difficult, proved to be a very rewarding task and I hope you enjoy the range of work that has made it to the final stages. With so many wonderful poems featured in this anthology picking a winner was another very difficult task so well done to *Grace Harris* who has been chosen as the best poet in this anthology. I'd also like to congratulate all the young writers featured in this collection.

Finally, I hope you find the poems that lie within these pages just as entertaining as I did and I hope it is kept as a keepsake for many years to come.

Warren Arthur

CONTENTS

Salenia Dodd (9)	56
Liam David William Lewis (9)	57
Freya Georgia Haynes (9)	58
Tyler Rochford (9)	59
Rhianna Jean Lloyd (9)	60
Darcy Aspinall (9)	61
Jayden Chikaonda (9)	62
Keira Lei Gore (9)	63
Darcie Blackburn (9)	64

Ightenhill Primary School, Burnley

Aiden John-Paul Shapcott (10)	65
Lucas Benson (9)	66
Jayden Daniel Carter (9)	67
Jessica Kemp (10)	68
Nathaniel Hill (10)	69
Chloe Francis (10)	70
Isabella Caddis (10)	71
Mason Dobson (9)	72
Reeze Lockett (9)	73
Charlie Ennis (10)	74
Denas Vilkauskas (11)	75
Nani Davies (9)	76
Harry William Crabtree (10)	77
Ebony Caitlin Robinson-Young (10)	78
Ryan Lewins-Eden (10)	79
Riley Jack Carter (9)	80
Sam Thompson (10)	81
Isobelle Violet Alderson (10)	82
Kailee Carter (10)	83
Dominic Zaibus (10)	84
Evie Swindlehurst (9)	85
Megan Stansfield (10)	86

Quernmore CE Controlled School, Lancaster

Abbie Sarah Woodhouse (10)	87
Tom Watson (10)	88
Seth Rainford (9)	90
Jad Ghazal (10)	91
Evie Hobbs (10)	92

Ruby Annabelle Moore (10)	93
Trinity Cresswell (10)	94
George Thackeray (10)	95
Olivia Winn (11)	96
George Davies (11)	97
Jake Hird (10)	98
Imogen Lily Haden (10)	99
Evalyn Greenall (9)	100
Oran Worgan (10)	101

Sacred Heart RC Primary School, Westhoughton

Aimee Olivia Tanner (10)	102
James Paul Hodkinson (10)	104
Aisling Maria McCabe (10)	106
Freddie Ritchie (10)	108
Lucia Lily Farrimond (10)	110
Phoebe Colley (7)	112
Grace Mannion (10)	113
Leigha Ann Towers (10)	114
Grace Lily Mulholland (10)	116
Arshia Saeed (10)	117
George Heaton (9)	118
Callum O'Hanlon (10)	119
Joshua Fox (7)	120
Isabelle Atherton (10)	121
Poppy Ashton (8)	122
Katie Coffey (8)	123
Jack Callaghan (10)	124
Zach Dixon (8)	125
Charlotte Newton-Harrison (8)	126
Finlay James-Wyatt (8)	127
Joel Strong (10)	128
Ishaan Saeed (8)	129
Tegan Cory (10)	130
Benjamin Lucas Callaghan (8)	131
Imogen Cory (10)	132
Heidi Gifford (10)	133
Miles Mather (8)	134
Benjamin Waterworth (10)	135
Summer Louise Southern (8)	136
Chloe Rowson (7)	137
Lewis Samuel Davies (8)	138

Sam Walsh-Ryan (8) — 139
Lewis Fletcher (8) — 140
Jack Paul Hodkinson (10) — 141
Henry Duffy (8) — 142
Samuel Thomas Cutajar (8) — 143
Mark Owen (8) — 144

St Anne's Primary School, Waterfoot

Phoebe Brown (10) — 145
Delilah Williams (9) — 146
Alesha Grace Howorth (10) — 147
Noah Pemberton (10) — 148
Poppy Pearl Millard (9) — 149
Jasper Heywood Clough (10) — 150
Seth Arthur Williams (10) — 151
Olivia Testa-O'Neill (8) — 152
Billy Partington-Duerden (9) — 153
Lily Anne Gooding (10) — 154

St Michael & St John's RC Primary School, Clitheroe

Willow Honour Mai Reynolds (9) — 155
Maya Krokowska (9) — 156

Trinity CE Methodist Primary School, Buckshaw Village

Eleanor Rose McKelvie (8) — 157
Evie Grace Taylor (8) — 158
Sophie King (8) — 160
Oliver Wheeldon (8) — 161
Daisy Stott (7) — 162
Jasmyne Holt (8) — 163
May Elizabeth McGowan (8) — 164
Imogen Aurora Moult (8) — 165
Annabelle Aldred (8) — 166
Millie Blackwell (8) — 167
Anna Williams (8) — 168
Chloe Quinn (8) — 169
Rithwik Narla (8) — 170

West Street Community Primary School, Colne

Nikita Broadbent (10) — 171
Haleema Mahmood (10) — 172
Maddison Butterworth (9) — 173
Owen Evans (10) — 174
Rose King (11) — 175
Scarlett Atkinson (10) — 176

THE POEMS

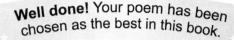

Well done! Your poem has been chosen as the best in this book.

Dreamland

Dreamland is the best by far
Although you can't get there by car
No, you have to go to sleep
Close your eyes and do not peep
When you get there you will see
Things that would not happen to be
Pigs can fly and flowers talk
The blind can see and the lame walk
As fast as lightning you can go
To anywhere you could possibly know.

When you wake up from that dream
From places that you've never been
Treasure that dream in your heart
And then it will leave its mark.

Grace Harris (11)
Quernmore CE Controlled School, Lancaster

City Of Books

In my dream I am in a city of books,
Where no one cares about your looks.
Brilliant sounds surround me,
Pop! Bang! are the sounds I hear, *bzzz,*
I hear the sound of a bee.

As I walked down another lane of texts,
I hear a racket like,
Ting-a-ling! Ring, ring! and a boy shouting,
'Stop, Mike!'

As I go further, I grab a book,
Open it up and out pops a witch.
She walks on,
I try stopping her from walking into a ditch.

A few streets away I see literature,
Where my favourite author is sitting.
She writes a book about a bandit who is terrible-
looking,
I go up to her, ask her a few questions.
With the courage of a lion,
I ask her to sign my most prized possession.

To the world I return,
My heart and soul will yearn.
Goodbye to you, city book,
I wish I could stand and look.

One day my dream will come true,
With a hot brew.
Book of City, I will adore,
Literature, texts and books galore.

Amina Hussain (10)
Al-Ikhlaas Primary School, Nelson

Jannah (Heaven)

I wake up and there's a light shining in my eye,
I didn't get to tell my mum goodbye.
I wake up with nothing in sight,
I wake up in a fright.

Rivers with milk, wine and honey,
It's so sunny!
Palaces made out of silver and gold,
I will never ever feel cold!

You will never ever feel tired,
You will feel pure,
You will never ever feel ill,
You won't need a cure.

You can eat things like cotton candy,
Have pets, I'll call you Randy.
The best of all, you will see Allah,
I love Jannah!

I feel as honoured as a king,
There is so much *bling!*
The prophets you will meet,
The prophets you will greet.

No frills,
No perils,
Amazing animals,
No perils.

Big fruits on trees,
Nice honey from the bees,
With rivers full of cream,
I dreamt my dream.

Eesaa Chaudhri (10)
Al-Ikhlaas Primary School, Nelson

Paradise, Paradise, Oh Sweet Paradise

Paradise is the only place,
Where you will want to race.
You will get a palace made of gold and silver,
This will never make you shiver.

You will get pearls so big and bright,
This will be a wonderful sight.
Everybody will be 33 years old,
This is something that we have been told.

There'll be three rivers, honey, milk and wine,
The wine will be sweet, delicious and taste just fine.
There will be such huge fruits,
They won't be wearing suits.

The birds will be singing in the morning,
You won't be groaning.
The prophet will meet us there,
None of the people will be spare.

You will be able to get a gigantic car,
In which you can go far.
You will get to see Allah's face,
And be surrounded by His Majesty's grace.

Talha Rashid (10)
Al-Ikhlaas Primary School, Nelson

Sheikh Mahir-Al-Muaiqly

Mahir-Al-Muaiqly is the Imam of Makkah,
Which is also called Bakkah,
He has very good recitation,
And is one of Allah's creation!

His face is diamond white,
And makes my life bright.
During taraweeh it echoes his voice,
And spreads through the peaceful night
When there is no choice.

I make dua that I see him very soon,
I want to go to Makkah before noon.
He is my favourite reciter,
And definitely is not a dictator.

Sheikh Mahir's voice everyone likes,
The four walls his sound strikes,
He has a fabulous voice, he does,
He has beautiful recitation, *he does!*

Sheikh Mahir-Al-Muaiqly is very strong,
He never reads the Holy Book wrong.
He is a famous reciter,
And makes my world brighter!

Hamaad Mehdi (9)
Al-Ikhlaas Primary School, Nelson

Jannah Tulfirdous

Jannah! Jannah! Jannah!
I would like to be in Jannah,
It's my dream,
I hope my dreams come true.

There are rivers made of honey, wine and milk,
I hope the dresses are made out of silk.
Jannah is really tall,
None of us will be able to fall.

Jannah will have a variety of different coloured cars,
Woo-hoo!
I hope I will have a good home,
That has lots of windows and dome.

In Jannah, the fruit trees will grow big,
And we will not have to dig.
Delicious the fruits will be,
Just picking from the tree.

My dream will come true I hope,
To Jannah I will get a rope.
Wow! The gardens will be a sight,
And we will not have to fight.
Jannah! Jannah! Jannah! I love you,
And I hope you love me too.

Farina Ulhaq
Al-Ikhlaas Primary School, Nelson

Getting Lost In The Jungle

What's that noise?
Thud! Thud! Thud! Rustle, rustle, rustle!
Hiding in the long green grass ahead,
Is this my imagination or for real?
Am I going to be eaten alive?
Uh-oh, quick, it's time to fly.

The creepy noise is getting nearer and louder
And I am becoming more afraid.
Do I run as fast as I can,
Or do I stay here
And become very brave?
I feel trapped in this nightmare.

I need to wake myself up,
Before the hideous tiger swallows me whole.
I scream a deep, frightened scream
As I slip gracefully into the tiger's mouth.

Suddenly, I wake up, sweating and terror-stricken.
I am in my soft, lovely, pink, glittery bed
With my sister, Amy.

Aishah Noor Hussain (9)
Al-Ikhlaas Primary School, Nelson

The Big Chance

F irmly, I stood in the middle of a pitch
O bscurely, I kicked the ball at the wrong time
O bviously, I thought, *what have I done?*
T he crowd were going mad as me and Ronaldo went face-to-face
B rilliantly, Ronaldo got the ball and scored in our net
A ll of the players in the other team were yelling, 'Goal!'
L uckily, there was more time left to score a goal
L oudly, the other team yelled, 'We scored a goal!'

M y heart said I could do it
A ll of my body said I could do it
T hen I got the ball and scored
C razily, my team yelled, 'We scored a goal!'
H ip hip hooray!

Eesah Yasir Miah (8)
Al-Ikhlaas Primary School, Nelson

Where Could I Be?

Where could I be?
I am awake with glee.
I'm not quite sure when this will end.
'What is that?' I ask.
I see monsters. 'Yuck!'

Where could I be?
I am not sure.
I open the blinds...
'What's that?' I ask unconsciously.
I spot a monster and a pixie!
'What could be happening?'

Where could I be?
I brush my teeth and guess what?
I catch a glimpse of a teacher
(Her teeth sticking out like a rabbit.)

Where could I be?
'Can somebody tell me!' I yell.
'You are in Dreamland,' says a famous pirate.
'What, no!' I shriek.
'Oh I am still in bed!' I exclaim.

Juwariah Sultan (11)
Al-Ikhlaas Primary School, Nelson

Candyland!

Candyland, Candyland!
It's the best place to be.
So many delicious candies,
Look here, look there,
Oh, so wonderful!

Gingerbread man climbing trees,
Chocolate fountain with marshmallow bees.
Cotton candy and clouds, yummy,
Rowntrees' gums bouncing on Mummy.

Galaxy mixing into the wafer,
No chocolate, no sweets are safer.
Ferrero Rocher melting into rivers,
And leaves me with lots of shivers.

Kinder joys are laid in a row,
To catch them you do not need a bow.
Terry's chocolate like a fireball,
Rolling from the mountain so tall.

Chocolate city, my dream cannot end,
I walk to visit my friends.

Aliza Fatima Majid (10)
Al-Ikhlaas Primary School, Nelson

Islam

Dreaming of being an Islamic teacher is
Just a dream come true,
I just want to do it because I want to spread Islam.

OK children, let's go and learn this deen,
And we need to get this keen,
You need to believe in Allah,
And then to pray Salah.

We should read a surah,
And fast on the day of Ashura,
But don't mention this to the surah,
To believe in Allah as one.

Masjid is the only place,
Where people gather for Allah's grace,
To believe in the prophets,
In order to gain many profits.

Come to the beautiful Saudi
But it's a bit rowdy,
Visit the holy places
And enter the Jarah palaces.

Billal Ali
Al-Ikhlaas Primary School, Nelson

Bismah, The Famous Female Footballer

I was on the green and white football pitch,
In front of the enormous goal pose.
The seats were full
And people were watching the game.
We were about to play.
I was on the red team
And once the game started,
I scored ten goals.
Everyone was watching anxiously
With their beady eyes
And clapping with excitement.
We won the match,
The next game was the finals.
Who said girls can't play football?
My team were very proud of me.
I was the only one scoring ten goals.
I was given £1,000 every day as the golden prize.
With the money I became famous Bismah,
The famous footballer.
I kept my shiny trophy on my shelf,
It looked amazing.

Bismah Chaudhri (9)
Al-Ikhlaas Primary School, Nelson

I Dream A Dream...

I dreamed a dream of a place so high,
Where flowers bloom and birds do fly.

The sound of silence is all you hear,
And the twinkling of stars so far, yet so near.

The green grass so luscious and fresh,
So smooth and soft where it touches your flesh.

I long to go there and hope and pray,
That this dream will certainly come true one day.

Yet I know for sure it's only a dream today,
But maybe, just maybe, it's not far off that day.

I dreamed a dream of a place so high,
Where flowers bloom and birds do fly.

Saaliha Shahbaz (11)
Al-Ikhlaas Primary School, Nelson

Ninja Go

I was walking down the street with my ninja team,
I saw robbers stealing from the bank.
I used my spinjitzu.
'Ninjas go!' I yelled.

My team used their powers.
Zane was a robot and was the master of ice.
Cole was master of earth.
Kai was master of fire.
Jay was master of lightning.
Lloyd was master of ice, earth, fire and lightning.
Skylor can steal anyone's powers by touching them.
'Ninjas go!'

How we do spinjitzu is easy.
All we do is turn into a tornado and move.
'Ninjas go!'

Huzaifa Razzaq (8)
Al-Ikhlaas Primary School, Nelson

Paradise

P laying so happily with my famous family
A mazed with what I see, standing on glass with multicoloured fish under me
R oaming around with fairies flying around me and my family
A sking for everything which is never-ending
D ull things are not alive, everything is shining bright like a diamond
I look to my right, I look to my left, I look down and I see rivers flowing beneath me
S o many beautiful things, I don't know what to do
E verything is so cool, it's like a wizard is making superpowers go everywhere.

Samiya Tasneem Hoque (8)
Al-Ikhlaas Primary School, Nelson

Once Upon A Dream!

I close my eyes and drift away in my dream

One, two, three, go!
I'm in a fairy land.
I don't know if I'm banned.
Ooh, some candy,
I don't know if it's actually real,
Let me take a bite.

I take a bite,
Everything starts to disappear
And turn into rock.
I'm with Mr Unicorn but suddenly,
We disappear.

I run towards the trees,
There you are, Mr Unicorn.
It has gone all grey.
He must have eaten candy too!

Aminah Mahmood (9)
Al-Ikhlaas Primary School, Nelson

Paint Galore

P urple is the colour of juicy grapes,
A mber when drivers are ready to go!
I ndigo is what aubergines are,
N ude is the colour of lipstick not seen,
T urquoise the colour of eyes you see with.

G reen means go, go, go!
A quas where the fish swim and plants sway.
L ilac, the colour of baby bluebells,
O range, the colour of tangy orangeade.
R ed is the oozing blood,
E merald-green, shining so precious.

Hafsa Asif
Al-Ikhlaas Primary School, Nelson

Heroic Heroes

S trong superheroes for the world
U nite heroes with special powers
P haraohs riding on fireballing phoenixes
E asy kills everywhere around
R oaring dragons fighting on the ground
H eroic heroes saving the world
E nchanting swords for more power
R aining and thundering, striking the ground
O wning some super weapons
E ntering a mysterious realm
S aving the world from evil villains.

Uzair Ansir (8)
Al-Ikhlaas Primary School, Nelson

New York Flying Wars

F antastic, brilliant, shiny, flying cars
L ovely cars, when I see them they make my eyes shine
Y es indeed, I love flying cars
I n the beautiful chocolate bars
N ow it's time for the flying cars to shine
G o flying cars, I hope I see you again

C onfident cars in the air
A ttractive bars with them
R un, run, they go
S o they roar on.

Hassan Mehdi (8)
Al-Ikhlaas Primary School, Nelson

Dragons!

D anger! Dragons have arrived

R ockets are terrible, dragons breathe on them

A thletes hate wizards, they turn them to lizards

G etting lost is very popular, where's my mother?

O ranges don't give energy, instead you breathe fire

N aughty dragons, you invaded our Earth

S uddenly, I found out I'm surrounded in my bed.

Muhammad Isa Abbas (9)

Al-Ikhlaas Primary School, Nelson

Good Days

G ood is nice, not even a thud
O rangutans are even finding their day good
O lympic players are getting so much money
D ogs have so much space

D ays are going good
A nd all shops are open
Y ay is being shouted with joy
S orry, but I'm out of paper.

Shoaib Abbas (8)
Al-Ikhlaas Primary School, Nelson

The Adventure Of The Jungle

I was skipping in my back garden
Someone said pardon
There was a monkey
With something funky.

I went into a jungle
I heard a rumble
It was a grumbling bear.

There was a wriggly worm
The worm squirmed
Its name was Feron.

Hanifah Shahbaz (9)
Al-Ikhlaas Primary School, Nelson

Dragons

D inner is here for dragons
R oaring across the burnt land
A ncient dragons fighting Vikings
G rowling loudly at each other
O utrageous blue and red dragons fighting
N oisy as a gorilla
S melly as a sock.

Qasim Ali (9)
Al-Ikhlaas Primary School, Nelson

Royalty

R acing to the finish line
O verjoyed queen with pines
Y ou are in a pit
A candle lit
L and of queens
T o make beans
Y es, of course this is Queen Street.

Manahil Sultan (8)
Al-Ikhlaas Primary School, Nelson

Cat

I am a cat,
I chase rats,
One day I went for a walk,
I began to talk.
Then I found out it was a dream
And I began to scream.
Then I turned all red
And I found myself lying in bed!

Maryam Rashid
Al-Ikhlaas Primary School, Nelson

Lion

L ost in a cage
I am on stage
O n a lion's head
N ow I see I am in a scary dream and I am in my cosy
bed.

Hasan Hussain (8)
Al-Ikhlaas Primary School, Nelson

Land Of Sugar

As I looked up and saw
my bed was made of candyfloss
I was at a complete loss
I just didn't understand.
Sheets of liquorice for a cover
I loudly yelled out for my mother.

There was fizzy juice as bath water
'Come quick!' I shouted out to Walter
At the door I saw a puppy dog
On the floor was a croaking frog
And gummy worms as pets.

There was a drawbridge of cake
Mint walls which were not fake
Pond and moats made of honey
Another pet was a chocolate bunny

I feasted my eyes upon the trees
They really were the bees - bee's knees
I saw ponies made of jelly
And a jellyfish with a big belly
Pigs made of strawberry ice cream
I never wanted to wake up from this dream!

Elizabeth Montgomery (11)
Castercliff Primary Academy, Nelson

I Won!

I looked at my numbers,
I had won,
My luck had just begun.
I was as rich as the Queen.
I could afford a limousine.

I could buy the latest cars,
Visit the famous stars
Go on holiday to France
Buy new designer pants
Get a mansion with a cupcake base
A roof with icing neatly placed.

Get the neatest clothes
Get asked to go on TV shows
Buy a rocket to the moon
It would make a loud zoom...
I'll buy a pet giraffe
It would have a funny laugh

I'll never have to go to work
Wouldn't that be fun?
I thought of all the possibilities
But I knew I'd have to think about relatives
It would be so cool.

Everyone would think I rule
I'd have an Olympic-sized pool.

I opened my eyes
I nearly cried
It was all lies
It was all in my head
However as I lay in bed
I would never forget
The dream when I won...
99 billion pounds!

Libby Thornton (11)
Castercliff Primary Academy, Nelson

Untitled

An island of a dream.
As I drifted off into a big dream
I saw leprechauns stood as part of a team
As small as ants the leprechauns skipped
But just then, I saw that one had slipped.

In the distance I could see a house,
And then I saw a little mouse.
All the house was made of was sweets,
It guessed it was time to have a treat.

Glaring at me the sun was bright,
It looked at me from its great height.
The sun reflected off the lake,
And it was time to take a break.

I opened the door and it let out a creak.
As I spotted him - I could barely speak
From the kitchen, I heard a cry
I couldn't believe I could see Jack Septic-Eye.

Connor Turner (11)
Castercliff Primary Academy, Nelson

Haunted House

The haunted house gave me such a scare
This was a lot worse than a silly nightmare
But wait... what was that - there was something there.

'Grrrrr!' cried the monster
'Rarrrrr!' yelled the ghoul
'Oh no!' I cried
This was not cool.

Drip, drip, drip, splashed the blood on the floor
Slip, slip, slip, plodded my feet on the floor
The candle flame danced and I heard another roar

Bang!
The door closed behind me
This was a scary horror film I needed to scream
Oh hang on a minute - it was all a dream!

Emily Credland (10)
Castercliff Primary Academy, Nelson

Sweet Treats!

This is my dream,
Chocolate sauce on ice cream,
All cool and sweet,
Wouldn't that be a treat?

Hair like cotton candy.
The beach is always sandy,
You can hear the trumpets,
But not smell the crumpets.

My house is made of sugary sweets,
Chocolate cakes and huge marshmallow roof tiles,
Surrounded by lollipop trees.

But the only thing is,
Where are the trees?
Bang, bang! What was that?
I just saw a gingerbread cat.

The wind sang,
The sun danced to the music of the alarm.
We have to wake up now and here we are.

Michaela Tonkinson (11)
Castercliff Primary Academy, Nelson

Winter Wonderland

Is that a dinosaur lumbering about?
Or is it just a gigantic sprout?
It looks like a humongous lizard
Oh great now I'm in a blizzard.

The wind is howling
Whilst bears are prowling
They're like a deadly disease
But really they're a soft species.

Santa is wrapping toys
For all the different aged boys.
The elves are preparing beautiful pearls
For all the different aged girls.

Throughout the Winter Wonderland
There was a professional band.
They played the fiddle
And told a complicated riddle.

Megan Jeffery (11)
Castercliff Primary Academy, Nelson

Horrid Nightmares

Giant spiders surrounded me, what would I do?
As black as death, they smelled like poo.

They edged closer to me so I began to scream.
How would I get out of this horrible dream?

Falling apart, they were right next to me.
Covered in bats and smelling like wee.

I banged on the door, I hoped someone was in.
It sounded like a zombie was rummaging in the bin.

The lightning roared not to be ignored.
Then I woke up in bed.

Ryan Poole (11)
Castercliff Primary Academy, Nelson

Riot In LA

Bang! There was a massive explosion
a huge mob ran out in slow motion
there was a riot in LA
everyone wanted to get away.

They were heading to a white house
they rode there on their big, bright cows
just then some cowboys came
and called all of the people lame.

Some then travelled back to LA
whilst the others went the other way
they made it to a white house
and they still rode on their big, bright cows.

Bailey Ellerton (11)
Castercliff Primary Academy, Nelson

Rabbit In The School

As I was sat in lesson
I saw a white rabbit run past
And the rabbit was running very fast.

As I got up from my chair
The rabbit was no longer there.
I followed him down the dark hallway
I really wanted him to play.

And then I fell down a deep dark hole
Crashing and tumbling, where would I go?
Could I get to Wonderland?

Seconds later I woke up from my dream.
'I want to go back to sleep!' I screamed.

Ellie Louise French (11)
Castercliff Primary Academy, Nelson

Dream Garden

My garden has colossal trees
And lovely flowers too.
It's all so pretty
With fresh grass that is pink and blue.

Oh my secret garden
I wish it would stay
for more than a day
If I had to give it someone
they would certainly have to pay.

My garden is amazing
I treasure it with my life
It's all so pretty
but oh what a pity

This was all just a dream.

Sam Woodruff (11)
Castercliff Primary Academy, Nelson

My Dream Garden

My dream garden
My house is made of candy
My grass is made of mash
My pond is made of gravy
My flowers wrapped in wrap.

My waterfall made of ketchup
My trees made of sausage
My branches made of chips
All chopped up into bikes.

The sun that's in the sky
Is staring down at me
Oh how I love my garden
And how my garden loves me.

Abby Fawcett (11)
Castercliff Primary Academy, Nelson

My Dream Life

I looked out the window and what did I see?
A beautiful star shining at me.
I came across another world,
Right in front of my face,
So I chose some clothes
And flew right into space.
I met two friendly fairies called Sparkle and Shine,
Their bloomy heaven was sparkly and beautiful.
But on one side it was full of darkness and gloom.
Smoke horns full of adventure and war,
All because one man had taken the heart of grace.
He had to return it, or all the smoke horns
Would fight our company of fairies.
It would be a shame to war!

Shona Melody Baker (8)
Gaskell Community Primary School, Bolton

Once Upon A Time Land

C hocolate falling on the floor
H e jumped into the house and made a bang!
O h, what a beautiful unicorn shining bright
C hocolate cars being eaten by people and unicorns
O h, a chocolate tree waving goodbye to you
L ate for chocolate school
A chocolate raindrop falling on your head
T ie your tie up
E lastic full of chocolate

L earn chocolate stuff
A chocolate food for dinner
N ana is the best
D ad is the best.

Javeriya Ali (7)
Gaskell Community Primary School, Bolton

In The Queen's Castle

A tree of glitter. I went in the air and could see a butterfly.

I saw a house in a life
M ay I come in your dream?
A super place to live
G rass full of flowers
I am in my best place
N ot impossible for a dream to come in a life
A glitter house
T ree can hear the sound
I am in my best dream
O nce upon a time I saw the Queen
N ot fair that I didn't get something to drink.

Maham Muhammad (7)
Gaskell Community Primary School, Bolton

Once Upon A Dream

F airies flutter all about in the land where the sun walks about
A ll of the animals are beautiful and magical
I t is a nice day when I see a rainbow unicorn, it is dancing
R eindeer fly and make their bells ring
I am surprised to see different creatures
E veryone in the world is excited to see me and the phones are dancing all over
S ee, what a colourful dance you do, what a big flash!

Aleeza Ameen (8)
Gaskell Community Primary School, Bolton

A Mission To Complete

S ave the children!
U nfortunately, we have to save the children!
P ersevere!
E veryone loves me
R ich is the only thing for pirates
P irates are the meanies!
O h no, pirates might win
W e need to save the children
E veryone needs to help by working together
R ight, let's work together
S uperpowers, that's what we all need!

Abdullah Kiani (8)
Gaskell Community Primary School, Bolton

Glitter World

Fairies, dancers and glitter unicorns,
My family in Fairyland, excited I fly.
I saw a big monster,
Astronauts, superheroes, clowns,
Wizards, dinosaurs and teachers.
The teacher was as blue as a blueberry.
Bang! Pop! Fizz! Whizz!
The teacher rolls along the grass.

Scarlett Jackson (8)
Gaskell Community Primary School, Bolton

Coming To Life

D reams are my favourite place to be

R emembering my dream from a long time ago

E verything came to life

A stone, a house, toffees and cups

M ost of the time I dream of getting back there

S hall I take you to my dream?

Max Mason Molyneux (8)

Gaskell Community Primary School, Bolton

My Dream

Fairies fly with special magic
Animals eat vegetables and meat
Young babies dance, fly and do some magic
The butterflies twinkle and sparkle like stars.

Frankie Naylor (8)
Gaskell Community Primary School, Bolton

Footballer

One day there was a man called Zlatan Ibrahimovic
And we turned into friends.
We were playing football
And after we played a penalty shoot-out,
We went to his house and played there too.
We invited a friend along.
His name was Wayne Rooney.
Then I invited David de Gea,
He was in goal.
I scored fifteen goals against him,
I even got a hat-trick.
Then they took me somewhere special,
A football stadium where there were fans all around...
Old Trafford.
Man Utd won against Man City 4-2
And I was pleased because I was at a stadium.
There was a happy ending.
I lived with Zlatan for a week, then went home.
I found myself in bed at home.
At the end, I was happy at home.

Bobby Hilton (8)
Hindley Green St John's CE Primary School, Wigan

Defeating Princess Ragdoll

I am in a candy world,
We're princesses but we're strong.
We're here to defeat evil,
We hope we're not wrong.

Our names are Paige, Cadie, Keira and Katy,
With the cutest weapons ever.
We are all the bestest friends,
We'll never break up, never.

We're here to defeat a rag doll,
A princess rag doll indeed.
We pass the candy farmers,
Planting lots of seeds.

We can see a castle,
A castle that's really big,
It is what we're looking for,
With guards riding pigs.

We are defeating a rag doll,
A very creepy one,
Now she is gone,
And we are moving on.

I find a weird portal,
And then I go through it.
I find myself in bed,
With my blue teddy called Pacific.

Katy Gregory (9)
Hindley Green St John's CE Primary School, Wigan

Nightmare Castle

I walk down a street and there is a door at the end.
As I walk, I look for a bend.
I take a glance back, the road behind is disappearing,
The door is appearing.
I'm getting closer, closer, closer,
I am passing out, I'm getting slower.
I get to the door,
The door is poor.
Inside there are kids,
Behind with their vids,
I've got to get them out somehow,
I am losing my eyebrows.
There's a girl getting electrocuted
And whatever, they are scared of getting tooted.
To the real world,
I was hurled.
I am with Tyson Fury, Muhammed Ali, Mantacore
And a lot more.
I am starting to get fed,
Then I wake up in bed.
Wooaahhh!

Jake Smith (9)
Hindley Green St John's CE Primary School, Wigan

My Biggest Fear

H elp me, I'm scared
E lf-like people everywhere
R un! Run! I say to myself
O h, help me, please
B ring help please, I'm gonna die
R un, I can't run for much longer
I know where I am, I try to survive
N o! No! No! Not him!
E very time I see this one room, I know it's his house
S urrounded by his fire, I am gonna burn to death

H im, it's him!
O h no, this can't be happening, not him!
U p and up I go
S omehow I'm in his house
E veryone meet my biggest fear, Herobrine.

Carson John Owen (9)
Hindley Green St John's CE Primary School, Wigan

Zombie Apocalypse And Spiders

I wake up in the pitch-black,
To find myself terrified of bats.
There is a chill running up my spine
And I'm beginning to wonder why.
I lift up my skirt but then I wish I didn't,
To find spiders as creepy as a ghost.
I get chased by a group of zombies in the dark.
After running for a thousand years,
I finally get to the end of this nightmare land.
I walk backwards to get away quicker,
But all of a sudden, the zombies and spiders disappear.
I fall into a dreaded hole,
Then I wake up and find myself
On the edge of my bed, ready for breakfast.

Lyla Crothers (8)
Hindley Green St John's CE Primary School, Wigan

The Ballet Dancer

B allet is what I love to do

A ll of the audience clap and cheer

L ots of audiences start to dance too

L ots of ladies start to come near

E veryone enjoys my bright smile

T o have a lot of fun

D ancing free is all I do

A nd I love everyone smiling too

N ervous yet excited I am

C adie comes to cheer me on

E veryone from school comes to support me

R ide a bike to see me dance.

Then I find myself back in bed, snoring away!

Aneira Llowarch (9)
Hindley Green St John's CE Primary School, Wigan

Dance Moms, BFF And Me

One upon a little time...

D ancing, dancing, dancing is that what I see? Is it dancing?

A n audience is watching me, oh my gosh, that's so cool

N o way, my best friend is here with Dance Moms

C limbing up a big wall, oops, I forgot, I'm afraid of heights

I knew I could do it, but how do I get down?

N o way, I'm famous at dancing, thank you Darcie, thank you Dance Moms

G osh, what a time I've had, everyone got mad but I found myself in bed.

Salenia Dodd (9)
Hindley Green St John's CE Primary School, Wigan

YouTube Land

In Dreamland I was walking with my friends Tyler and
Cooper,
But when we were walking, we saw a YouTube building.
We went into it and we saw Repo and DanTDM.
We all went to see them.
When they saw us we recorded an FX video.
I was nervous, scared and happy.
When we got out of the room,
The walls were made of money
And we got it all before anyone else could.
Then we got a huge mansion.
It was white and black and I got super famous.

Liam David William Lewis (9)
Hindley Green St John's CE Primary School, Wigan

Famous

I walked down the red carpet and I saw pop stars.
A lot of them were millionaires.
I spoke to Taylor Swift, it was really a big twist.
She didn't know what to say.
Fans were crying,
Some spying on the new dress I gave away.
People were worried but the bodyguard was hurried
That nobody was getting over.
I was amazed that people were giving things away
For photos and bunnies.
It was really funny.
Then it ended!

Freya Georgia Haynes (9)
Hindley Green St John's CE Primary School, Wigan

Creepy Clowns

I woke up in darkness, I was scared.
Then I heard a clown laugh.
I was shaken, so I got up and ran.

I hid in my closet,
Cooper was in the closet, then the bell rang.
Cooper screamed.

Katy jumped out of the window
And landed in the pool.
Then she climbed the ladder and knocked the ladder over,
Destroying my Lamborghini.

Katy saw Paige and Cadie,
Then the clown was arrested.

Tyler Rochford (9)
Hindley Green St John's CE Primary School, Wigan

The Upside-Down Universe!

U pside-down universe
P ut birds in my face
S urround me with an emerald-green sky
I f I'm good, can I eat the clouds
D ecide tonight
E njoy my company forever

D ucks are now above my head
O ver my hair, the flowers grow in the green sky
W hen I walk on clouds I feel free
N ever forget me, I'll be back, don't forget.

Rhianna Jean Lloyd (9)
Hindley Green St John's CE Primary School, Wigan

Sing!

I stand in an arena as big as the sky.
I sing all day and all night.
I can see a loud, crazy crowd screaming very noisily.
Spotting me, my family and friends,
I can hear them cheering very loud.
I feel nervous, yet lively.
Come along and sing with me.
I love my audience, so do you love me?
I become the best pop singer
And I stand, singing as best I can.
Live, love, sing and sleep all night.

Darcy Aspinall (9)
Hindley Green St John's CE Primary School, Wigan

The Minecraft World

M ining things to create something cool
I feel excited by what I'm going to do
N othing is getting in my way except building
E verywhere
C rafting more items to build
R unning everywhere to find objects
A iming to make my first house ever
F orgetting what to build and getting hungry
T hough I'm nearly done, but I'm tired.

Jayden Chikaonda (9)
Hindley Green St John's CE Primary School, Wigan

Killer Clowns

K iller clowns everywhere
I n the forest meeting Borris
L ying and buying
L earning and killing
E ager to Norris
R unning for Borris

C hilling and billing
L earning and killing
O wning and phoning
W ining and dining
N ine bleeding dogs
S inging, 'I'm coming to get you!'

Keira Lei Gore (9)
Hindley Green St John's CE Primary School, Wigan

Brataley

Here in Brataley, I feel thrilled wherever I am.
This is a dream, this is incredible,
Or am I dreaming?
Annie and Hayley come running to me.
I feel so happy.
I wish this was real.
We put on our bathing suits
And splash into the pool.
We do gymnastics all day long,
Until we get starving!

Darcie Blackburn (9)
Hindley Green St John's CE Primary School, Wigan

Superheroes

I am a superhero, I am flying,
If anyone gets in my way, I will be denying.
Your name might be Joe,
But one more sleep and I will break your toe.
My name is Dan,
I will beat Superman.
From underdog is San
And I can kill Batman.
Oops, stop playing Dobble
Because someone is in trouble.

Now I'm on my way flying,
I think the villain is crying.
I see someone in a flower,
Now I am the person up on the tower.
The villains are going,
The citizen is falling.
The villains did invade
And it was the citizen that I saved.
The villains are going to their lair
And I get promoted by the mayor.

Aiden John-Paul Shapcott (10)
Ightenhill Primary School, Burnley

Footballer!

I wanted to be a footballer and that came true,
When I met the footballer at the zoo at half-past two.
I got his name, when we went to the club,
We had something to eat
And that was football cake!
So after that, we played at Turf Moor,
We won a trophy waiting just for me.
So we went to sleep with a snack.
The next day we played a match with my favourite team
And that team wears claret and blue.
It is Burnley, who are in the Premier League,
Which is the biggest football league in the world.

Lucas Benson (9)
Ightenhill Primary School, Burnley

My Dream

Pass me the ball,
I'm clean through,
I will score a goal,
You will hear their fans too.

I have finally got the ball,
I'm definitely not passing it
Because I can score a goal,
I've totally smashed it.

I can hear my fans roaring
Because I scored a goal.
The time is closing,
I get the last touch of the ball.

It has finally come,
It is time to run.
I have accomplished my dream,
I have won the Premier League.

Jayden Daniel Carter (9)
Ightenhill Primary School, Burnley

The Stage!

I'm on a stage,
Looking quite good for my age.
Crowds are going wild.

What is that?
Is that Postman Pat?
Oops! My mistake.

Singers, YouTubers next to me,
Ooh, this is exciting,
I think I'm going to pee.

They give me an award,
'Uh, I'm kind of getting bored!'
But wait, what's that noise?

Boom! Crash! The monsters say, 'Hi!'
Oh my goodness, I think I'm going to die.

Jessica Kemp (10)
Ightenhill Primary School, Burnley

Nathaniel Hill

N othing has prepared me for this strange land I see,
A t least I'm not as scared as can be.
T he shadows loom around me,
H earing my cries.
A shadow even has eyes.
N owhere to run, nowhere to hide,
I t trembles right inside.
E vil starts to overwhelm,
L urking in my mind.

H ow will I escape,
I 'll die if I don't.
L et me drift away,
L et me be OK.

Nathaniel Hill (10)
Ightenhill Primary School, Burnley

Nightmare

Goes into town, sees a clown,
Steps on a mouse with a frown.
The mouse died, so I drowned in my own tears,
Then I peered through a door that was on the floor.
The core of the Earth started to shake
And buildings started to quake.
The Earth started to break,
So I wanted cake.
Somebody baked it,
So then I could take it.
Before my life ends, I bend some pipes
And acid started spitting.
I finally got my cake,
But died of pneumonia.

Chloe Francis (10)
Ightenhill Primary School, Burnley

Singer

Dreaming in my bed,
It's flowing through my head.
People cheering me, I am proud,
But when I turn around,
I see something that is amazing.
It's my favourite band, I am cheering.
It's Little Mix, my favourite band.
I wish I could see them, but I am banned.
Suddenly, I win the awards.
So proud of myself,
Done well to get here,
But the worst thing has happened in my head,
I wake up in my bed!

Isabella Caddis (10)
Ightenhill Primary School, Burnley

Football

I could hear the crowd roaring
And the away fans were boring,
As I came through the tunnel,
The opposition were moaning.

My best friend passed it to me,
So I ran through and got the number three.
Fortunately for me,
My teammates paid for my tea.

I don't know what position to play,
I just want to be a footballer one day.
My dream has come true,
Well done to my teammates too.

Mason Dobson (9)
Ightenhill Primary School, Burnley

Becoming A Footballer

My teammate slotted it through,
But I got tackled by an angry kangaroo.
I want to be a footballer,
But I need to get a better ball.
If I need to be fast,
I need to dash like The Flash.
If I go in goal,
I need to be tall.
I don't know what position to play,
I just want to be a footballer one day.
I've got to get better,
'Cause I'm not quite that good yet, so don't put a
bet on.

Reeze Lockett (9)
Ightenhill Primary School, Burnley

The Clown

One day I saw a clown,
Whose mask had a frown.
It scared me on the street,
He also had huge feet.
I ran out of his way,
But he chased me for six days.
When I finally got away from him,
I ran into my bed.
I thought that by now,
The clown could be dead.
I woke up in the morning
And found out it was a dream,
So I fell asleep again
And that dream was rather keen.

Charlie Ennis (10)
Ightenhill Primary School, Burnley

Fly Back To The Galaxy!

I saw a big pirate ship,
It was full of pirates.
A dragon was flying high above
And from space
An astronaut came out of nowhere.
It made the pirate ship fly.
The scientist's experiment exploded,
It made the astronaut fly back to the galaxy
And out of the universe.
After a few minutes,
There was nothing but darkness.

Denas Vilkauskas (11)
Ightenhill Primary School, Burnley

My Haunted Neighbour

My neighbour is scary,
But not very hairy.
This guy has secrets I can tell,
If I find out that'll be swell.
Curiosity killed the cat,
And I'll be next, I can promise that.
I'd like to find out what he's hiding,
Won't be the last time he caught me spying.
Should I go say hello
Or should I just say goodbye?

Nani Davies (9)
Ightenhill Primary School, Burnley

Halloween

H allow halls closing in

A room not far away

L osing speed fast

L onger the hall keeps going

O h no, surrounded

W ill I ever get out?

E ventually I'll get out

E ven though the pumpkins are moving and the hall is black

N o one should come, just go far, far away.

Harry William Crabtree (10)
Ightenhill Primary School, Burnley

The Dream I Had One Night

I'm with my mother at the Magical Palace,
Watching the queen and her guards.
Then a peculiar fellow comes along
With a wand in his hand
And a cloak on his shoulders.
He puts up his wand and shouts,
'Abracadabra!'
The queen ends up as a witch,
But she still has a crown on her head.

Ebony Caitlin Robinson-Young (10)
Ightenhill Primary School, Burnley

Trouble On Earth

One day I was on a space mission,
But I got zapped by solar energy.
So I had to go back to Earth.
It was purple so we went to look
And we got attacked by dragons,
Killer clowns, wizards and monsters.
My horns were glowing
And sparks came out of my hand.
The population was down to two!

Ryan Lewins-Eden (10)
Ightenhill Primary School, Burnley

I Want To Be A Footballer

I want to be a footballer,
But I need to get taller.
If I want to be fast,
I need to dash like Flash.
If I want to score,
I can't be poor.
If I have to save,
I need to be brave.
I don't know what position to play,
I just want to be a professional one day.

Riley Jack Carter (9)
Ightenhill Primary School, Burnley

Spooky Aliens

One day on Mars, I was looking around,
Then an alien came to me out of a hole.
I talked to the alien, but the alien ran away.
So I ran after the alien.
I went back to the ship and let the alien go.
The alien ran back to its hole and I went home.
When I got home, I had tea.

Sam Thompson (10)
Ightenhill Primary School, Burnley

Night-Time

N ight-time

I s dark

G reat for slumber, but my bed is too

H ot

T o sleep in

T iredly

I said to

M yself

E ven the bed bugs say, 'Night-night.'

Isobelle Violet Alderson (10)
Ightenhill Primary School, Burnley

Dancer

A dancer, a prancer, what a morning!

D reaming in my bed,
A lways in my head.
N early awake,
C learly a dread.
E arly up in the morning,
R eally, it's boring.

Kailee Carter (10)
Ightenhill Primary School, Burnley

Footballers

If I want to be a footballer
I have got to be fast
If I want to be a footballer
I have to have tricks
If I want to be a footballer
I have to do well in school
If I want to be a footballer
I have to be smart.

Dominic Zaibus (10)
Ightenhill Primary School, Burnley

Athlete

A nd the crowd goes wild

T o see me win

H aving a blast

L aughing like it never lasts

E very day

T o help me on my way

E veryone will have to pay!

Evie Swindlehurst (9)

Ightenhill Primary School, Burnley

Teacher

Teaching early,
I doze in my bed,
Almost time to get up,
What a dread.
I wake in shock in my lovely bed,
Knowing I have to go dancing.

Megan Stansfield (10)
Ightenhill Primary School, Burnley

Joyful Jelly Land

J elly Land is super
E veryone has fun
L iving in their jelly huts
L ying in the sun
Y ou and I are different

L iking different things
A nimals are like Haribos
N ever stopping still
D ancing in the ice cream pool

I cy and ever so cool
S trawberry flavour jelly, jumping up and down

S lap! went the gummy bear playing with the pig
U sually parties last all night but this one's already been about two days...
P robably everyone will ask for more, more, more!
E veryone loves it, including you and me
R emember how I said everyone has fun. Well I had fun in this dream even though I've never been.

Abbie Sarah Woodhouse (10)

Quernmore CE Controlled School, Lancaster

The Derby

It's match day!
I feel the pressure
I'm Barca's top scorer
Their front three is deadly
It's Real Madrid
My Bugatti Chiron is roaring like a lion
I arrive just in time
Toot!
The ref's whistle sounds like a siren
The match ball was jumping for joy with eagerness to start
I cross it into Suárez
He hits the crossbar!
My heart sinks with frustration
Toot! (It's half time)
It's just ten minutes into the second half
Ronaldo gets the ball
He shoots, he scores!
Now we are on a dangerous attack
Neymar crosses the ball with the precision of a machine
My heart beats faster as I celebrate the equaliser
We're into stoppage time
I have the ball and it's now or never

The pressure feels overwhelming
Ramos is closing in
His tackle is as brutal as a cheetah killing its prey
Penalty!
The Barcelona crowd are expecting something special
The keeper is protecting its goal like a mother bird
protecting her nest
I'm planning to take a risk...
Suddenly everything stops
I can only hear my breathing
Slow and heavy like a whale
Everything seems in slow motion
I chip the ball
The keeper dives to his right
The ball holds its breath
And hits the back of the net, *boom!*
'Goal!'

Tom Watson (10)
Quernmore CE Controlled School, Lancaster

Jurassic Park

I walked through the world of dinosaurs
The first thing I saw was the biggest one ever
Thud! Thud! Thud!
I heard footsteps but louder than any man's
I turned round, I saw a dinosaur the size of a
skyscraper
The foot was the size of a man
Pop! Sounded like someone got squashed

I decided to carry on with my tour of the place
Screech! The sound of another dinosaur

Worriedly, I woke up as soon as possible and ran
straight to my mum and dad's room.

Seth Rainford (9)
Quernmore CE Controlled School, Lancaster

The Perfect Poem

Last night, I had a dream
That I made the perfect poem
It had similies and metaphors
And personification too
It had worlds of wonder
Which had bangs of thunder
All on a piece of paper.

Last night, I had a dream
That I made the perfect poem
The snowflakes danced
And the sun smiled down
While cooking its evening meal
The moon is my bedside lamp
While I lie down on my floating bed
Last night, I had a dream
That I made the perfect poem.

Jad Ghazal (10)
Quernmore CE Controlled School, Lancaster

Dreaming Is A Strange Thing

Dreaming is a strange thing that no one understands,
But when you go to bed in Dreamland you will land.
Where rainbows give you piggy backs and flowers chat
to Old Man Jack,
The fish are like jumping beans, diving up and down
And the grass says, 'Ow!' as hedgehogs' spikes prickle
on the ground.
And you'll wake up like always, peaceful in your bed,
But something will be different - you could be standing
on your head!

Evie Hobbs (10)
Quernmore CE Controlled School, Lancaster

Once Upon A Dream

The snowy cats jumped in the air and danced back
down
As the golden syrup lion took the crown
The blueberry seals were making deals
And the butterflies were eating chocolate pies
The sausage dogs were cooking in the oven
As icy penguins rolled down the hills of Duven
How I love this world so much, the elephants can speak
Dutch!
But as I enjoy this world it seems this world is just a...
Dream.

Ruby Annabelle Moore (10)
Quernmore CE Controlled School, Lancaster

Town In The Stars

I sat on a cloud and began to fly
Like a bird swooping high in the sky
I went into the stars past Jupiter and Mars
Then I came into a floating town where chimney tops
Were made of chocolate and let out purple smoke
I flew past the gingerbread houses and I waved to the folk
I went out of the town and saw some rainbow waterfalls
They splashed and danced into a stream
I woke up, it was all a dream.

Trinity Cresswell (10)
Quernmore CE Controlled School, Lancaster

Apocalypse

I was walking through a maze of chocolate.
Accidentally banging my head on colourful, dancing
gumdrops.
The birds sang beautiful songs, the catchy tunes
pulsing through my ears!
The tiny puppies charged around licking my shoes and I
ran as fast as lightning when it sprayed pebbles from
the heavens above!
It was wonderful.
But that was before the apocalypse...

George Thackeray (10)
Quernmore CE Controlled School, Lancaster

Magical World

In my magical world, happiness falls upon me
The sun shimmers like a sparkly chandelier
The rain falls like blue beads from the sky
Fruit and sweets come alive at the click of my fingers
My magical coconut squirts out rainbow milk from its
stripy straw
The clouds make my imagination go wild with all the
pictures they make.

Olivia Winn (11)
Quernmore CE Controlled School, Lancaster

The River Of Death

Through the river of death you go
The blood fighting for their land
The forest of graves
All watching you
Planning their revenge on you
For killing their friend!

Then you stop at a redwood tree
And you find the flowers
All dried up
It's OK, it's just a dream!
Wake up! Wake up!

George Davies (11)
Quernmore CE Controlled School, Lancaster

The BMX Racer

Racing round the rapid race track
On my one-gear BMX
The black bars burn like the sun
The salty sweat like seawater in my eyes
The wind whistles like a farmer calling for his dog
My wheels scream while going round the bend
I can smell victory
The trophy is in my sight!

Jake Hird (10)
Quernmore CE Controlled School, Lancaster

Once Upon A Dream

In a dream on an island,
The rabbits poo jelly beans.
The unicorns have candy canes as horns.
The BFD fires out hot chocolate
from his massive mouth
The beautiful gingerbread houses
are covered in colourful sweets.
I will treasure this dream for evermore.

Imogen Lily Haden (10)
Quernmore CE Controlled School, Lancaster

The Fantasy Dream

Dreamland is a dream
Unicorns eat pizza all day long
Sheep are like clouds in the sky
Swimming pools are Yorkshire puddings with gravy in
Tall trees twinkle like tinsel on the Christmas trees
This is my tremendous dream and I will treasure it for
evermore.

Evalyn Greenall (9)
Quernmore CE Controlled School, Lancaster

The Silver Sword

The moonlight shone off the silver blade's diamond hilt
It danced around the darkness
The blade jumped to and fro the falling soldiers
It swooshed through heads and bodies
It soared through the air like a skilful ballet dancer
The silver sword.

Oran Worgan (10)
Quernmore CE Controlled School, Lancaster

The Howling Horn!

In a dream world far, far away from here, a unicorn named Jet was on an adventure to save someone or something
He was off to do this for his own personal horn!
You have to complete the full mission to find a horn for him
A baby foal off on a dangerous mission to Rock Cannon
Each different unicorn had a different pattern for its magical horn
Depending on what you save and how
I was always told that there was a pot of gold, but seems to me that it was sold
No leprechaun, no gold, just unicorns dancing on rainbows
But sadly in the corner Jet was a loner
Those mean and nasty unicorns leaving poor Jet out
They are as grumpy as a bull!
We set off on our journey through the tightest of squeezes and the smallest of spaces
It was a journey with no turning back to Mummy!
The moon was screaming with moonlight whilst the daring devils bellow in the wind
Were we safe or was there danger up ahead?
A castle in sight of me and Jet

It had cobblestone bricks and green moss hanging
down the walls
All made of rotten hard candy
Were we ever going to get Jet's horn and complete the
mission through the hallow halls...?

Aimee Olivia Tanner (10)
Sacred Heart RC Primary School, Westhoughton

Me Playing In Front Of Millions

I'm nervous about playing in front of millions of people against an unbeatable team
Manchester City
Who are unbeaten in 44 games, me and my old friends from school
I am only 17 years old and playing in front of 100 million fans
My team would have to pull off a miracle to beat them
I need to play well when I'm playing for this amount of people in the stadium
Never mind the people watching on TV
It is very scary playing football for 100 million people
And so the game begins, it is amazing from the opening whistle
It is an amazing atmosphere
After twenty minutes we are 1-0 up, it is mind-blowing and my team are amazing
I am proud to be the captain of this team
After twenty-two minutes of playing, we score another goal, this time it is me who scores
I am so happy
Just before half time I score my second goal and we are 3-0 up, it is a dream come true
The second half starts and we score straight away, this time it isn't me who scores, but I'm still hunting for that hat-trick

'Will it come?' I ask myself
It was the last minute and finally I...

James Paul Hodkinson (10)
Sacred Heart RC Primary School, Westhoughton

Courage Can Make You Fly!

I arrived in a land called Sweetville
And what a horrible sight
A bunch of angry horses giving a unicorn quite a fright
They pushed her, kicked her and called her a freak
That made the unicorn upset and very, very meek
I really wanted to help her
I really, really did
But she went away screaming like a little kid

I found her sitting in the middle of a cave
I told her, 'I can listen sweet unicorn and I can hear
I can see you crying sweet unicorn
I can see you very clear.'
She said, 'I don't quite fit in because of my strange
horn
I've had it since I was a child ever since I was born.'
'You're beautiful like a rose
We're all different like a blade of grass in a lawn
You're amazing my sweet unicorn
You're original and unique
You're sensational my sweet unicorn, there's no need
to be meek

So fly away my sweet unicorn
Go as far away as you need.'
Suddenly she flew away never again to be seen.

Aisling Maria McCabe (10)
Sacred Heart RC Primary School, Westhoughton

The Home Of Football

I fell from the sky
The very first thing I saw was a sign saying
'Welcome to Football Landia'
'The home of football!'
I felt strong and powerful and felt ready for something
I can't find the word to describe the feeling
Sensational is nowhere near to the feeling's description
Never mind
I wanted to start running for some odd reason
So I did
I ran at the speed of light
I couldn't stop
In the distance was a crowd
I was so confused
Why am I running, why am I here? I thought
They started to chant my name like I was a celebrity
'Freddie! Freddie! Freddie!'
What is the meaning of me being here?
I'll try not to get into that
I may as well enjoy it
In the distance was a goalkeeper net
Questions ran through my head

All of a sudden, a ball appeared
I had one idea, my idea was to shoot
Then I woke up...

Freddie Ritchie (10)
Sacred Heart RC Primary School, Westhoughton

Riding Rainbows

At the end of a rainbow there was supposed to be gold
Well, that is what I'd always been told
But that was not a sight I saw
All I saw was a unicorn's horn
It smiled and shimmered in the light
Like a diamond in the night
It must have been waiting for someone to catch sight
Could it have been
No, not to me
I ran down to see if it could be
It sang a harmony I think, to me
So I grabbed on just to see
Riding rainbows upon candyfloss clouds
It was even hard to see a house
From high above the misty clouds
Red, yellow, green and blue
What an astonishing sight to me or you
I was nearly there at the end of its light
Maybe tomorrow day
Or maybe tomorrow night
I would see you in your light

Riding rainbows in sour-spray rain
Raspberry flavoured rain in my game
Pink, orange, purple and blue
They would be here to watch over you.

Lucia Lily Farrimond (10)
Sacred Heart RC Primary School, Westhoughton

Once Upon A Dream Tokyo...!

I dreamt that one day I saw a flying yummy bear, a flying fairy and an upside down unicorn.

I'm also in Dream Tokyo that has a lot of children's dreams in dream jars.

I'm on my way to the park in Dream Tokyo and then *bang! Thud!*

A weird shape of footsteps are marked in the mud inside the forest.

I was as scared as a deer in the headlights with my friends, Harriet, Zara, Summer and Katie.

Just then a face stared at us in the forest, it was a... big, hairy and hungry gorilla.

All of us were so, so, so scared because we have never ever seen a gorilla in our entire lives.

We ran as fast as we could, but the gorilla just kept chasing us and chasing us.

So I thought for a moment, if we ran out of the forest the gorilla would stop chasing us and he did.

At the edge of the forest we stepped out and sat on a comfy log.

After that I got up and found myself cosy in bed.

Phoebe Colley (7)
Sacred Heart RC Primary School, Westhoughton

Sweet Land

As I wonder where I am
I see a river made of maple syrup
With pink and purple boiled sweet boats bobbing on
top
I look up, I see cotton candy clouds
There's bubblegum trees and rock houses
And strawberry milkshake swimming pools that people
can drink
Only then did I realise I was in Sweet Land
My brothers went wild eating everything
Even the green sugar coloured grass that grew on the
ground
This is surely and truly Heaven for every child
'There's sweets everywhere!' my brothers screamed
With mouth and hands full of gummy bears that smiled
at you
There was a pile of mint chocolate chip leaves next to
every tree
'There's sweets everywhere!' we all screamed.

Grace Mannion (10)
Sacred Heart RC Primary School, Westhoughton

Once Upon A Nightmare...

It's a magical place in Magic Land
The rainbows are as bright as a light
Unicorns dance all day and night
No need to fret because magic's here
On our way to save the day
The greatest day of all time is here
Until that hour I disappear!
It's like my horn has come to life
I'm stuck in a world of dull and boring
Maybe I will never get back
Maybe the stars won't dance again
Will I ever see Cupcake the fairy
Or my friends again?
My magic is not powerful if don't unite
My once upon a dream became a once upon a
nightmare
Until I meet a loner
Who was sent here with a kaboosh
They send me back
With a little fairy dust
Didn't work!
Let's rewind that
They send me back
With a little fairy dust

I am back home
With Cupcake the fairy
Woohoo!

Leigha Ann Towers (10)
Sacred Heart RC Primary School, Westhoughton

My Pet Unicorn

My pet Usain Bolt unicorn, with the rainbow hair
Voom, she sped past the aeroplane
The people down below are as small as ants
The clouds up above are hitting me as I fly
I sometimes feel lonely but my unicorn makes it better
Swish, the unicorn's hair slapped me on the cheek, but I
didn't care
I went over the rainbow, I saw the leprechaun
I hoped to see the pot of gold
But no one was there
The shimmer from my unicorn's horn shone so brightly,
I squinted
I saw from my squint, the Starbucks sign
We fled past the drive thru
The shop was pulling me closer
I looked down at my hand to see
A unicorn frappucino waiting for me!

Grace Lily Mulholland (10)
Sacred Heart RC Primary School, Westhoughton

The Magical Land

I slowly crept in without a sound
Through the emerald-green leaves
Dark flowers looked at me all around
I started to regret the choice I made
But I waited to see
I walked and pushed away the leafy curtain
A white as cotton bright light blinded me
It was something fishy, I was certain
But really what could it be
I tried to see past the bright light
And then something sparkled more
I had to see what was so bright
There it was, something so beautiful
I hadn't seen before
The clouds were dancing in the air, so elegant and so fair
It was a magical land with unicorns, rainbows and chocolate rivers
Because it was a dream come true.

Arshia Saeed (10)
Sacred Heart RC Primary School, Westhoughton

Chicken Mystery...

In Candy World, everything was upside down
The sky was as green as an emerald
Then something mysterious flew across my face
It was a chicken!
But not any type of chicken
It was a chicken detective!
It had super cool shades on
And a really splendid hat
I crept up on it and it went *cluck, cluck* into the muck,
muck (which was chocolate)
The clouds were made of candyfloss
And birds chirped at our feet as loud as a car engine
I had a chocolate cake house, a profiterole chimney
and a white chocolate door and melted chocolate
windows
The chicken detective then ran because he saw his
villain, the Grinch
He was never to be seen again.

George Heaton (9)
Sacred Heart RC Primary School, Westhoughton

Howl In The Night

I look around and see a wolf
I stare at it with quite a big gulf
I look at myself and find a tail
When out of nowhere I hear, 'All hail!'

I was a wolf with such great claws
With a crown on my head, I got a round of applause
'What is this?' I say
They reply, 'You're our master and we're happy from
this day.'

I heard a howl, an alarm bell rang
When all of a sudden there was a great bang!
We need a defender, 'Attack!' I say
We have no fear from now on today.

We may be scared tomorrow, but I am in charge
At least until tomorrow, we are large!

Callum O'Hanlon (10)
Sacred Heart RC Primary School, Westhoughton

Flash The Football Fox

In the world of foxes, not so far away, is the stadium of
the Football Foxes
The very best player in football.
Foxes team was Flash, he went *zoom! Zoom!*
He was just like a car.

Famous fox has a house made of candy.
The floor is made of squishy, pink candyfloss and the
tap does drip with Fanta coming out of it.
The best are the Skittles coming out of the chimney.

One day, Flash went to play football with his friends
It was a penalty shoot-out and Flash was taking the
last penalty to win
He scored and united the Foxes
They won the shiny trophy and were given a mighty
monstrous medal.

Joshua Fox (7)
Sacred Heart RC Primary School, Westhoughton

Me And My Mum

I hit the ground
I close my eyes to find I am lying on candyfloss
Candyfloss which is as soft as my bed
Rapidly I jump off my heaven onto the ground
Surprised to feel a hard rock under a jaw-breaker
In the distance, I can see a flawless fairy
My eyes open wider and wider until they feel like
they're going to pop out
I slowly walk over, I smile, I see a glittering coming from
behind me
Her wings show a glow
I turn my head, she does the same
'Wings, wings, I have them!'
The light reflecting off them is as bright as sunlight
My wings look like a frosty icicle reflecting off glass.

Isabelle Atherton (10)
Sacred Heart RC Primary School, Westhoughton

Candylandy Landy Land

Once upon a dream, in Candylandy Landy Land
I was in my hard toffee, coffee bed
I woke up and my unicorn was on my lolly-polly toilet
I got up and saw my fairies
I said to myself, 'Where's Polly Fairy?
Oh, she's gone because of the Dragon Land!
I shall go and defeat the dragon with my unicorn with
their powers
And my powers too!'
There she was in Dragon Land
I saw the dragon and said, 'Oh, my full grief!'
'We did it! Yay! Now let's go here and have some
grass.'
'OK, let's go!'
We got into the Jacuzzi and ate McDonald's

Poppy Ashton (8)
Sacred Heart RC Primary School, Westhoughton

Once Upon A Dream

C otton candy trees, when they rustle at night they give me a fright

A ngry gummy bears stomping up and down 'cause they want to gulp porridge

N utty Kinder for me, pouring into the bath and enjoying

D ummy gummy suckers suck me like a baby, suck, suck

Y o-yo Winders, they are my noodles for tonight

L and on marshmallows, jumping from the candy plane

A nd the butter and syrup pancakes, mmm yummy!

N utty butter for Candy Land in the morning

D ummy gummy bears are happy now!

Katie Coffey (8)
Sacred Heart RC Primary School, Westhoughton

Football Crazy

I want to play football, I think I'm good
I'll ask that man over there in the hood
If he says yes, I guess I can play
He let me play, but I made a mistake, I kicked the ball
into the hay
I guess I'd better run away
I ran to the edge of the woods
I saw three men in dark black hoods
I went to ask them who they were
And one of them shocked me, it was Drogba
He was balancing a ball on top of his head
I wonder which school book he read?
The other two did not reveal
And one of them did not look real!

Jack Callaghan (10)
Sacred Heart RC Primary School, Westhoughton

Once Upon A Car

Once upon a car there was a special land of cars in a secret hole in Spain
The hole was a tiny hole
There was a boy who lived in that land named Zach, he loved cars
He had a Ferarri that went *zoom!*

His house was a fancy garage with a tiger couch and a leather bed
It smelt like a fresh breeze flowing in the air
It had peach curtains and a red carpet too.

One day his car ran out of fuel and the only way to get fuel was to win a trophy
He raced and won a trophy, 'Yes!' he cried.

Zach Dixon (8)
Sacred Heart RC Primary School, Westhoughton

Looking After Animals In Fairy Land

I can see lovely, adorable, cute, kind, gentle, careful pets and a huge, steamy, rough dragon with sparkles on it
In a Fairy Land with cute fairies and cute dragons, lots of pets and an ice queen
A fairy with lots of magic dust and all of the animals in Fairy Land become superheroes
I am with fairies, dragons, animals and an adorable ice queen witch to guard stars twinkling in the sky
I feel amazed, excited, surprised and shocked because the animals keep dying, I was upset
All of the fairies healed them and they came back!

Charlotte Newton-Harrison (8)
Sacred Heart RC Primary School, Westhoughton

Castle Land

I can see a king and queen sitting in their chairs with gummy bear guards and Oreo dogs.
I am up in the archery tower with David Beckham and my friends Luke, Sam and also Bill Elf.
I feel quite scared, but I'm not alone.

The castle door has a jaw-breaker door, football pitch roof and hard granite walls.
Fanta comes out of the door.
The king and queen are asleep and a robber comes and tries to rob.
Thud! the castle gate is down
Luke goes in for the attack and kills him.

Finlay James-Wyatt (8)
Sacred Heart RC Primary School, Westhoughton

Crazy Land Of Sweets

In my sugary sweet house
On my chocolate fudge chair
I was eating a chocolate mousse
And pulling out my liquorice hair
Under my gingerbread roof
In my caramel bath
I looked at my window
To see a big crack, as big as a building
The candy cane trees danced in the wind
The sugary sherbet coated bush too
Waved at me from my caramel bath
If only I had my sugary teeth
Oh how amazing it would be
But they all fell out due to my Candyland of sweets
Oh how the sugar mocks me.

Joel Strong (10)
Sacred Heart RC Primary School, Westhoughton

Massive Musical World

I live in a massive musical mansion in a massive
musical world
There are musical clouds, instrumental ground and
colourful animals roaming around

When I was walking down the instrumental path, *thud,
thud, bang!*
The massive, mighty monster sat down crying and
made everything sad and soggy

Then I came to realise that he just wanted to be friends
We made friends and the massive musical world was
back
I felt scared but when we made friends I was happy
once again.

Ishaan Saeed (8)
Sacred Heart RC Primary School, Westhoughton

Love Is A Rainbow

When my love is upon your hands you will know how
much I care for you
Bluebells are blue, roses are red, I will flee with you
You have a heart of gold that gives me warm hugs
every day
A golden crystal of locks reaches my lips
If I imagined an angel I think it would look like you
You are my truest love today, you are an angel and a
darting crystal at bloom
My heart will stay with you, my gorgeous
Love is you
You are my snow angel in winter and my flower in June.

Tegan Cory (10)
Sacred Heart RC Primary School, Westhoughton

Life In Ponyville

P onies are everywhere

O n they run twirling and whirling everywhere

N o pony doesn't have any friends, all of them have buddies

Y ou would like to live here, there are all sorts of people to meet and lots of things to eat

V olleyball is the most popular game there

I t's the best in Ponyville, I hope you

L ove it too

L ove one another, it's what we do

E veryone will be your friend, including me too!

Benjamin Lucas Callaghan (8)

Sacred Heart RC Primary School, Westhoughton

Candy Land

Everything's chocolate and sweets in Candy Land, even
the cherry-coated grass with liquorice ducks swimming
in the caramel stream
The jumping jelly bean frogs hop around in Candy Land
My house is made of cookies and cream, ice cream, it
stays together with the sticky strawberry laces and the
chocolate chip cookies
The door is made out of chocolate crackers and the
windows are made out of lollipops! Yum!
Might just have a lick
My house is delicious and I ate it all!

Imogen Cory (10)
Sacred Heart RC Primary School, Westhoughton

Meeting The Monster

D ark moon is watching me

I n the darkness shining a bright shiny star

N ight-time has come closely, followed by danger

O nly the brave dinosaurs can kill the monsters

S ave the love of her life, Alfie

A lfie is big and strong. He can pick up an elephant

U gly dinosaurs are watching me

R oaring dinosaurs moaning around me

S tomping dinosaurs! *Stomp! Stomp! Stomp!*

Heidi Gifford (10)
Sacred Heart RC Primary School, Westhoughton

Crime Town

Once upon a dream there was a man named Miles
And his best agent, Dan, and the clown chase began
It was a day that started like any other day
Until clowns were everywhere
'Let's go out!'
'OK.'
'Move out of the way or you may get shot.'
Use the GPS to track them down
'Where are there around us.'
'There's a trap.'
'Pull it.'
'Mission accomplished!'

Miles Mather (8)
Sacred Heart RC Primary School, Westhoughton

Rally Car

R acing round a sandy track
A s quick as a flash
L iving the dream
L inking the twin turbo
Y ou and I racing round a track

C lear windscreen to see the sandy, soggy track
A fter racing, winning the golden trophy
R evving the engine, finished racing

Going round a rack
Every time going smack
With a body rack
Smashing the back.

Benjamin Waterworth (10)
Sacred Heart RC Primary School, Westhoughton

Wonderland!

Once I dreamed I was a magical fairy princess with a
pet unicorn
I dived into a big pales, I slept on a fairy princess bed
It was as pink as a pig
The carpets were as fluffy as a sheep
My palace was made out of glass and wood
My garden was beautiful, it had lots of roses
My unicorn had a big stable and my fairy also had a
little home in my palace too
They love it when the melted chocolate came out of
the taps.

Summer Louise Southern (8)
Sacred Heart RC Primary School, Westhoughton

Once Upon A Dream

Colourful unicorn flying in the sky
Drip, drip off the chocolate, tasty tap
Yummy candyfloss floating in the blue sky
Unicorns are magical at making flowers
Mum unicorn is making yummy goldfish
Terrifying, evil unicorn lives in a dark, evil world
Exciting goldfish and exciting huge castles
Open and closed, *bang!* the doors slam shut
Best candy and chocolate on the marshmallow ground.

Chloe Rowson (7)
Sacred Heart RC Primary School, Westhoughton

Once In Pirate Bay

Once, when pirates were there, a big creature slurped
out of the sea
His tentacles were as long as trees, so they took their
swords out and they hit with *slash* and *bam!*
They then went back to sea and found Blackbeard's
ship
Boom! went the cannons
They used the plank which was as thin as a stick
Blackbeard's tiny ship sank to the bottom of the ocean
and off they went to sea.

Lewis Samuel Davies (8)
Sacred Heart RC Primary School, Westhoughton

Ping Pong World

I see Whizzy McSquizy, Dragoon my pet and a bad,
scary dragon
I live in Ginger Jolly Hut where everyone is jolly
Whizzy is short, Whizzy McSquizy who lives in Liquorice
Lair with liquorice for life
Dragoon lives in Ginger Jolly Hut with me
Bad dragon lives in Stone Stove Cave where it is all
stone and iron with 200 stoves
After that, Dragoon gets giant because of Whizzy and
kills the big, bad dragon.

Sam Walsh-Ryan (8)
Sacred Heart RC Primary School, Westhoughton

Once Upon A Dream

In Football Land you can see all the stadiums in the
world
All the trophies in the world, all the players in the world
You are in Football Land, the home of all football
Every century in the world, every nation in the world
Every team in the world
It's amazing
I'm with Sergio Ramos, Ibra and Messi
And people do freestyling on the street or in stadiums.

Lewis Fletcher (8)
Sacred Heart RC Primary School, Westhoughton

Candylicious

As I take a candylicious treat
It melts off my finger and sticks to my mouth
Now I know it takes a beat
But all I need is a finger-licking treat

It might seem all right to eat
But actually it's not just that
It's also fabulous to meet
I might seem in defeat but all I need
Is a candylicious treat.

Jack Paul Hodkinson (10)
Sacred Heart RC Primary School, Westhoughton

Dream Land

D reams are very exciting so we're going into one
R oman gummies are attacking the nuts
E normous candy, ice cream and Mrs Gummy Bear
A rtist sprouts
M armalade lorries

L and is very scrumptious here
A mazing mazes
N aughty nuts
D angerous pear drops.

Henry Duffy (8)
Sacred Heart RC Primary School, Westhoughton

Wonderland

Dreams are made by powerful magical wizards
They make an infinite source of them so you have an infinite store of dragons
They are made as pets, they only spawn in Candy Land
I live in the Candy Land
I can see candy canes on my doorstep and my massive candy house
My wizard friend is here, wow, he's created my grand pet dragon.

Samuel Thomas Cutajar (8)
Sacred Heart RC Primary School, Westhoughton

Speedy Dolphin

Sometimes the sun was burning hot
Unusually, my best dolphin was extremely fast
Next I went to my tasty house that smelled like pizza
And waited for the shark to show up
A nice, sunny day, I saw a super fast shark
Now the ocean was calm, I went to the middle of the ocean
Delighted, because I caught the shark.

Mark Owen (8)
Sacred Heart RC Primary School, Westhoughton

Nightmare In An Unknown Place

S piders climbing up the walls

P laces I have never been, where am I?

O h look, there's so many webs at least they're up high

O h my gosh, is that a giant spider? Oh why?

K aitlyn, why is she here and why is she being chased by a spider?

Y uck, is that slime from a cobweb? Yuck, this must be a dream

S pooked to death, me and Lily

P eeking around every corner spiders everywhere, wait, where's Lily?

I n this place why are there so many bends?

D ining spiders eating a girl named Megan

E yes glow of evil red lurking in the shadows

R ed eyes follow my every move like a bat

S uddenly I wake to find I'm in my bed at home safe and sound.

Phoebe Brown (10)
St Anne's Primary School, Waterfoot

Help!

Once I was in an enchanted forest where all my fairy
friends lived
My fairy friends always told me if trouble was
approaching
But usually when I come, no trouble was coming
One spooky night where the wind was howling
My unicorn, Starfire, was as beautiful as a princess
She was right beside me until lots of smoke filled the
room
And suddenly
A giant dragon appeared, sending me and Starfire into
doom
I opened my eyes, thinking I was in a dragon's dungeon
But really I was just in my bed fast asleep
Happily I got out of my bed
Ready to start the day
I wish that dragon was friendly to all my fairy friends
Even me!

Delilah Williams (9)
St Anne's Primary School, Waterfoot

Pleasant Devil!

Pleasant devil, pleasant devil, where are you?
Pleasant devil, pleasant devil, what do you do?
Jumping out behind the wall
Jumping out in the hall!

Walking through the mall with Mum
Strolling in the park to run

Every night I go to bed
I always dream you in my head
But then I wake up in my bed
I always wonder what you said

We always roll the big, white dice
For tea we eat curry and rice
You creep around just like mice
We always try to find the best price
But every time you ring the bell
I know I'll carry on sleeping well!

Alesha Grace Howorth (10)
St Anne's Primary School, Waterfoot

Sweets

S leeping... sweets, chocolate and candy
W hen I saw it, all I did was...
E at and
E at
T hen I was as fast as a pig
S eeing him made me jump

A fter, I made sure he didn't see me
N ow, when he saw me, I slapped him
D ancing on the floor in pain

C andy Man was scared of me
A nd then I really knew it was a dream
N ow I was sad because it was dawn
D own in my dream, means down in the real world
Y awning, no my dream is gone, but it's not always.

Noah Pemberton (10)
St Anne's Primary School, Waterfoot

My Magical Unicorn Dream

I can feel it in my toes
I can feel it in my bones
It's swishing in my hair
There's definitely dream magic in the air

There's a magic horn on my head
The colour of my horn is the same as baking bread
There's a dream swishing in my head as I lay in my bed
There's noise like a creak, it's coming from a stable shed

I'm standing on four legs
I walk louder than hatching eggs
My nose is as wet as rain and as black as the night sky
I am a unicorn and I'm going to reign a dream world as I fly.

Poppy Pearl Millard (9)
St Anne's Primary School, Waterfoot

Spiders Swallow

S neaking up on me slowly like a sloth
P icking the perfect time to run
I gnoring all fears like a lion hunting
D reaming in the night sky
E motional as a romantic movie
R unning for my life
S lowly running out of breath

S urrounded by trees
W hat to do next
A lone with only one place to go
L osing balance like a drunk person
L ying down on the ground
O n top of the building
W aking up slowly feeling ill.

Jasper Heywood Clough (10)
St Anne's Primary School, Waterfoot

Dream Away Boy

D reams are wonderful
R esting in the night
E ating all your ideas
A re you tucked in tight
M ay you sleep well little boy!

A way with the stars as bright as an angel
W icked witch or a beautiful butterfly
A way you go to the world of fun
Y ou cute little guy

B ye-bye dream, you say in the day
O ff you go downstairs
Y ou lay back in bed to go far away after a cold winter's day.

Seth Arthur Williams (10)
St Anne's Primary School, Waterfoot

My Dancing Dream

I'm dancing freely, my wish has come true.
As elegant as the water, flowing down a stream.
I think I'm in bed, but I know I'm not.

Now I have finished my dance,
I go to my team.
We shout and scream, that's our way of celebrating.

I hear an alarm and only I hear it.
I knew it was just a dream.
Now it's time to wake up.

Olivia Testa-O'Neill (8)
St Anne's Primary School, Waterfoot

Football Dream

F ootball is my favourite sport

O n my feet are my best football boots

O n my body is my favourite kit

T ip: always use spikes

B urnley is my team, hopefully we will win the league

A ll the best teams are in the Premier League

L ost, we go into the changing room

L ast night I dreamt that!

Billy Partington-Duerden (9)
St Anne's Primary School, Waterfoot

The Happy Dream

I just love this dream
Right now I am eating ice cream
So many unicorns
I love them all
Wow, this is a giant hall
This house is as big as a castle
What's that rattle?
It's a baby unicorn!
So cute
What's that noise?
Hello kitty cat
Do you like my hat?

Lily Anne Gooding (10)
St Anne's Primary School, Waterfoot

The Adventures

All of this is making me amazed
I hope the magic won't make me dazed
Here in the Magical Kingdom
The unicorns are full of wisdom

Me and Ruby go to a dance studio
One of the girls is called Julie

Me and Lucy are at class
In the middle of class, someone is playing the brass
School, school, school not so cool
Stay in school
Don't be a fool!

Willow Honour Mai Reynolds (9)
St Michael & St John's RC Primary School, Clitheroe

Fairy Land

F ar off in the distance

A s I see some sparkles

I see a little, lovely fairy land

R eagana is a famous fairy and Willow is a queen

I notice fairies love to fly on unicorns

E very fairy has his own power

S ee the colours of the rainbow shining through your window.

Maya Krokowska (9)
St Michael & St John's RC Primary School, Clitheroe

The Magical Phoenix

Once upon a dream I was a beautiful phoenix
I dreamt I made an aeroplane out of sticks
I got inside and flew really fast
I saw an alien's spaceship that whizzed past
I felt there were butterflies tickling my tummy
I stopped with a halt and at Disney World was a
mummy
Then I heard a screaming roller coaster ride
I felt I wanted to scurry and hide
Suddenly a vampire stepped behind me sucking blood
I ran to a desert island, there I stood
I was surrounded by turquoise, wavy sea
I heard a busy, buzzing bee
I found a delicate, precious locket
And put it in my lucky pocket
By the noise of the swishy, swirly whirlpool
I was drifted back to my desk at welcoming school.

Eleanor Rose McKelvie (8)
Trinity CE Methodist Primary School, Buckshaw Village

Once Upon A Dream

Once upon a dream, I was flying
High, higher and up into the sky
Once upon a dream, I couldn't fly
I had no superpowers, they had all gone, bye-bye.

Once upon a dream my powers were back but not
flying tonight
This time I was Mystery Jack!
Finding the answers and looking for clues
I'm the best detective and I like the blues.

Once upon a dream, I was a professional dancer
Spinning and twirling, I got a ten from Len!
Once upon a dream, I had two left feet
Clumsy and falling, I'd never dance again.

Once upon a dream, I played a mermaid called Ariel
In an underwater film, I even had fins!
Once upon a dream, or was it a nightmare?
I was scared of the water and wouldn't go in.

Dreams can be hopes, wishes or nightmares
They're very different
They could be false, they could be true
You could always win or always lose.

There's never two the same
I like how every night they change
It's like a never-ending story book
Running through my brain.

Evie Grace Taylor (8)
Trinity CE Methodist Primary School, Buckshaw Village

Anything Is Possible When You're In A Dream

I close my eyes and drift off to a faraway place
It is ace as I stare, beaming into space
I mysteriously fly by all stuff that could be possible
All I see for a minute is mystical, floating fairies
You are in luck because an astronaut with electrical powers
Is saving the world from a man-eating monster
A wizard is casting a spell on Mars to be cold as it is too hot
Then I see a graceful ballerina dancing on the moon
In a flash a super, shooting star comes flying past
But I am scared of getting lost because I don't know which way to go
I close my eyes and I am in my warm, cosy bed
Anything is possible when you're in a dream.

Sophie King (8)
Trinity CE Methodist Primary School, Buckshaw Village

The Flying Football

One day I set foot on the World Cup Final pitch that looked like it was from the century of 1901, in a chocolate egg!

F irst I thought of scoring so that's what I did
O h my, what a great goal it was
O w, how my ear drums hurt
'T ry to keep down the noise!' I said
B alls were flying and I didn't know which one to kick
A ll I wanted to do was bag another one home
L eaving the game, what a sight
L ose or win, score a goal, that's the match and that's all.

Be proud if you win or lose because you tried your best and that's all that matters.

Oliver Wheeldon (8)
Trinity CE Methodist Primary School, Buckshaw Village

The Spooky Shipwreck

Lying abandoned on the sand
A ship that once was very grand
In a blink of an eye I saw it there
Shall I take a closer look? Do I dare?

I took a step forward and saw a light
As it flashed in and out
It gave me such a fright
I touched it gently and heard it creak
It scared me so much, I let out a shriek

I saw a chest full of gold
Which filled me with glee
As I saw it there staring at me
I grabbed the gold so greedily
But I saw someone watching, so I ran away speedily
Then I woke up to find it was a dream
Don't worry, I wasn't scared in this scary dream.

Daisy Stott (7)
Trinity CE Methodist Primary School, Buckshaw Village

The Secret Unicorn

S ecret unicorn, see me again

E verybody knows you inside their heads

C ome on out, I want us to play

R esting too long underneath my bed

E verybody knows that I want to see you again

T oo many things we could do for you

U nrevealed creature you are the perfect image in my head

N o way I will leave you again!

I want to play outside with you and never forget

C ome on we can't be late

O h no! We're not going to get there

R ight now we are not going to be late

N ow we see ourselves again!

Jasmyne Holt (8)
Trinity CE Methodist Primary School, Buckshaw Village

When I Grow Up...

When I grow up...
I want to be an astronaut, so I can watch the moon brush the surface
I want to be a hairdresser, so I can brush and curl this
I want to be famous or a movie star, *click*, there goes another camera, *click, click*
I want to be a ballerina, twist, turn, leap and bow
I want to be a teacher, ooh let's make this class fun
I want to work in a bar, actually I think I'll pass!

But I want to be a writer because then I can write my own dreams.

May Elizabeth McGowan (8)
Trinity CE Methodist Primary School, Buckshaw Village

Police Officer Puppy Names

My puppy, what would she be called?
On the lead she might be pulled

If she was called Anna, would her favourite food be a banana?
If she was called Puppy Officer, she might turn into a Cookie Officer
If she was called Sofia, would she be a sphere?
If she was called Criminal Biter, would she pull her coat tighter?
If she was called Millie, would she be silly?
If she was called Dotty, would she be spotty?

So many names
Is this a game?

Imogen Aurora Moult (8)
Trinity CE Methodist Primary School, Buckshaw Village

The Ballerina

Ballerina, Ballerina, dreaming of Paris
Whilst living in a palace

Often she thinks of performing in pink
To people all around

She performs on her toes, so everybody knows
How she dances and moves her way

As she twirls and swirls while wearing her pearls
She is the best dancer amongst all the girls

The people are amazed as she dances through a maze
The sun beams down as the ballerina bows.

Annabelle Aldred (8)
Trinity CE Methodist Primary School, Buckshaw Village

If I Was Called...

If I was called Bobby, would you ask me my hobby?
If I was called Immy, would I have a chipmunk called Chimey?
If I was called May, would I say hey?
If I was called Anna, would I have a banana?
If I was called Rio, would I have a brother called Leo?
If I was called Maisie, would I be hazy?
If I was called Mollie, would I have a lolly?

But I'm called Millie and I'm very silly!

Millie Blackwell (8)
Trinity CE Methodist Primary School, Buckshaw Village

Anna's Ballerina Dream

Miss Lucy's clapping
I'm happy
The lights are tapping
The other class are being snappy
We twist and turn with a smile
Our coach is watching
The other class is trying
Their coach is dodging them
The Palace Theatre is excited
Their coach is annoyed
Our coach is delighted
The other class is destroyed
And we have won!
Just then I wake up and I am back in the boring world.

Anna Williams (8)
Trinity CE Methodist Primary School, Buckshaw Village

The Happy New Year Song

We had some fun, but it's past the day
But in this dream, I will have to just play!
Inside this dream, I will be with my best friend, Lilly
Which is also a bit of silly
A lot of people, there was a crime
Which is going to be in a rhyme
Lilly went looking with her sight
But suddenly, we found him bright
Then it was solved by me and Lilly!

Chloe Quinn (8)
Trinity CE Methodist Primary School, Buckshaw Village

My Dragon

M y dragon is only very small
Y ou might not know about this little creature of mine

D oes he sound scary?
R obert, my dragon, can be very fiery
A t home, he likes to play
G rab him carefully because he might bite you
O n my bed he plays
N ow he is behind you so get out of the way!

Rithwik Narla (8)
Trinity CE Methodist Primary School, Buckshaw Village

Fairy Tale Dreams

My eyes start to droop
And my dreams start to loop
I'm in Slumberland, a wonderful place
With the other fairies I race and play chase
My ornate butterfly wings
Are elegant violet glitter things
In the distance: among pearl pink, sunset orange, silky
clouds the fairy castle gleams
And I am overcome with wondrous fairy princess
dreams
The studded butterfly crown sits on my head
Not a single salty tear is ever shed
Gold dust fills the evening air
Swallowing my brown limp hair

Boom! Crash! The bad nightmare wipes away my fairy
tale dream
All fairies flee with a tiny, scared scream
I run on the clouds as a man.... Dailey Bad Dream
chases me

Is this really how it must be?

Mr Dailey shouts that I have my head in a cloud
He says I have detention for a week and he's not
proud.

Nikita Broadbent (10)
West Street Community Primary School, Colne

171

Nightmare

N ight-time is when things come to life, my heart stops and my imagination turns on

I magery fills my head and fills me up with bizarre things

G ory dreams swallow me up...

H orrified, I whisper in my sleep

T eeth hooking memories, pulling me to bed

M ysterious thoughts drenching my head...

A stonishing eruptions bursting with fear

R evolting things cascade into one

E motions swelling up in my head!

Haleema Mahmood (10)
West Street Community Primary School, Colne

Evacuee

E nvious I was when I was e...

V acuated from across the l...

A nd scary houses around frightened be...

C ause I had never seen animals before crying for my m...

U m, wanting to leave, I don't want to be an evacu...

E e, it's scary and it's a nightmare you s...

E e and it's a scary and tormenting nightmare.

Maddison Butterworth (9)
West Street Community Primary School, Colne

Superhero

S uper strength, sonic speed
U pon me, I do good deeds
P ranks of villains are too easy
E ven if you fly you'll feel queasy
R eal people get scared too easily
H eroes like me win confidently
E vil people deserve to go to jail
R ivals lose, but I don't fail
O h no, they're in trouble!

Owen Evans (10)
West Street Community Primary School, Colne

Mermaid

M y lips are bright red

E verywhere the beautiful blue sea

R ed coral on the seabed

M y legs are a tail with golden curls to match

A mazing shades of blue, aquamarine

I must be dreaming

D reaming, yes I am!

Rose King (11)
West Street Community Primary School, Colne

Fairy Drama

Waking up surprised
My wings are like a butterfly
Oh no, they've fallen off
Now I'll look like a moth
They turned crisped brown
And fell to the ground
They're no longer colourful
And now they're not beautiful.

Scarlett Atkinson (10)
West Street Community Primary School, Colne

Est.1991

YOUNG WRITERS INFORMATION

We hope you have enjoyed reading this book – and
that you will continue to in the coming years.

If you're a young writer who enjoys reading and creative writing,
or the parent of an enthusiastic poet or story writer,
do visit our website **www.youngwriters.co.uk**. Here you will
find free competitions, workshops and games, as well as
recommended reads, a poetry glossary and our blog.

If you would like to order further copies of this book,
or any of our other titles, then please give us a
call or visit **www.youngwriters.co.uk**.

Young Writers
Remus House
Coltsfoot Drive
Peterborough
PE2 9BF
(01733) 890066
info@youngwriters.co.uk